P9-CLJ-109

DISCARDED
PLC
2012

JUL 29 2003
MAIN

JUL 2 5 2002

MAIN

NEW CALIFORNIA POETRY

EDITED BY

Robert Hass
Calvin Bedient
Brenda Hillman

The publisher gratefully acknowledges
the generous contribution to this book
provided by Joan Palevsky.

GONE

UNIVERSITY OF CALIFORNIA PRESS   BERKELEY   LOS ANGELES   LONDON

poems

FANNY HOWE

GONE

University of California Press
Berkeley and Los Angeles, California

University of California Press, Ltd.
London, England

© 2003 by The Regents of the
University of California

Library of Congress Cataloging-in-
Publication Data

Howe, Fanny.
Gone : poems / Fanny Howe.
p. cm. — (New California Poetry; 7)
ISBN 0-520-23624-6 (alk. paper) —
ISBN 0-520-23810-9 (pbk. : alk. paper)
I. Title. II. Series.
PS3558.O89G6 2003
811'.54 — dc21
2002038728
CIP

Manufactured in Canada

12 11 10 09 08 07 06 05 04 03
     10 9 8 7 6 5 4 3 2 1

The paper used in this publication meets the
minimum requirements of American
National Standard for Information
Sciences — Permanence of Paper for Printed
Library Materials, ANSI Z39.48-1984. ♾

All this day I have been in a dream, half miserable and half ecstatic: miserable because I could not follow it out uninterruptedly; ecstatic because it shewed almost in the vivid light of reality the ongoings of the infernal world.

CHARLOTTE BRONTË

CONTENTS

ACKNOWLEDGMENTS

Lots of thanks to the editors of those magazines who printed some of these poems first—including *Conjunctions, Hambone, Fence, Columbia Poetry Review, Washington Square, Syllogism, 26, Volt, Seneca Review,* as well as a+bend and shifting units presses and *Best American Poetry 2001.*

THE SPLINTER

When I was a child

I left my body to look for one
whose image nestles in the center of a wide valley

in perfect isolation wild as Eden

till one became many: spirits in presence

yes workers and no workers up on the tops
of the hills in striped overalls

toy capes puffing
and blue veils as yet unrealized in the sky

I made myself homeless
on purpose for this shinnying up the silence

murky hand-pulls
Gray the first color
many textured clay beneath my feet

my face shining up I lost faith but once

(theology)

To stay with me
that path of death was soft

this pump's emotion
irregular, the sand

blew everywhere

My hands were tied
to one ahead

driving a herd to the edge

(mother)

She said I said why

fear there's nothing to it
at any minute
a stepping out of and into
no columns no firmament

Most of each thing
is whole but contingent
on something about
the nearest one to it

Confused but moving
the only stranger I know
has a bed a blanket
a heartfullness famous
for hypocrisy

When she's not trusting anyone
she leans her crown
upon her hand
snowslop all the way to the grating
before lying down

in a little block of childhood
(one hour for the whole of life)
and her book to record it

Was the chasm between her mind
and things

constituted by the intellect's catalogue
or by the presence of senses
(around her face

objects fall into special functions

tangled loops against concrete walls
moonish nuclear fission capped with molten gold)

or by a sticky sub-atomic soul

See how this being at the neck and bowel
gives the head and groin a taste of hell

that seeps throughout some nervous systems

all senses battered and enflamed

where the soul drinks disabled

and attacks only a she a she can see
who smiles in dreams between clenched hands

sobbing from wanting to win her pity
her in the born-hating

thing she finds there living

(Skin is what I she and they see when we see feelings)

Not I but a she-shaped one
over fluid frame

sized to capture what comes in

agony that heaven doesn't begin

(to know the soul imprinting is in pain)

Short of being nailed but sure of being labeled

now my name is forced now her name is first
into my ear my hearing her not being

here so I will know that this is the hour
when I will have to hear her

named and cringing rise
to the utterance

as my own excruciating presence

Very pain it came first
through my eyes
they were so compressed
I could still see
forms that will never be
eliminated and illuminations
and words whose imprint
(branded in agony)
still can't be interpreted

Coal is the first sign of a wreck

that your face may blacken
with bliss of the night

Recognition

You can hide
from whoever is red enough

with force or sex to make you sad

The history of the defeated

Eternal lie
as if to prove
the principal
root of the verb
to falsify
is life
itself an excess
since whoever is
identified
is already buried
while staying still
will show what nothing is

So if her skindeep faith
could stay intact
and the original forgery is genetics
and lies increased belief
then was her brain always seeking
the right word
to show that consciousness
does die in places
out of range of her own flesh

Last night I hated her
when I was what she saw in her mirror

and rage can only be appeased by praise

(the winning world backs in on you this way)

Does she mean what she says
or do statements form on her lips

Does she mean what she says
or do statements rise to her lips

If it is she then I exist
but if the words are mechanistic

then they can only be read
by reversing images

(the urge to hurt her emerges)

She grew to dare herself to murder that
which worked to murder her
and murder what was birthed to murder her as I also
aspired to murder
slaved and longed to murder her name
my own murderous member

This way my always unquiet mind would clear its one evil
would not go to sleep insane
After all should I become a fate
like any other not if she can remember
not if she could reconnoiter those faces better faces
now strained through her hate where a woman
among them wonders Why can't I be like her and hate her

(The globe is a brain
It always believed it had no right to life
Its father was its mother

After the blessing came the naming
and accounting for the birthing order)

Where I grew life
and died as a little apple

—forget nipping and chewing—

I stopped she dropped
beside an especially long worm

the balls of her feet aching
somewhere out in the rain

one of those rains that blink until dawn
with the eyes behind them

Depression in the sea
a heavy day
unbecoming anything
after the hope
that drags behind
the one she doesn't want to see
or waves away
cruelty always more credible

The holes in our haloes
widen the higher we die

(a light snowfall
the airport stilled)

And just a pane away from a face

one glove is waving

All our provision gone to waste

So the first shall be lost
and the zero before it

and the weight of faithless skin
shall thicken its authority

in a mind fired by a spark

whose intake of breath is automatic
until it isn't

Winter spears
its buds of snow
until a white rose
bleeds gold and trembling
and barely visible
(artificial)
two at a windowpane

DOUBT

Virginia Woolf committed suicide in 1941 when the German bombing campaign against England was at its peak and when she was reading Freud whom she had staved off until then.

Edith Stein, recently and controversially beatified by the Pope, who had successfully worked to transform an existential vocabulary into a theological one, was taken to Auschwitz in August 1942.

Two years later Simone Weil died in a hospital in England— of illness and depression—determined to know what it is to know.
She, as much as Woolf and Stein, sought salvation in a choice of words.

But multitudes succumb to the sorrow induced by an inexact vocabulary.

While a whole change in discourse is a sign of conversion, the alteration of a single word only signals a kind of doubt about the value of the surrounding words.
Poets tend to hover over words in this troubled state of mind. What holds them poised in this position is the occasional eruption of happiness.

While we would all like to know if the individual person is a phenomenon either culturally or spiritually conceived and why everyone doesn't kill everyone else, including themselves, since they can—poets act out the problem with their words.

Why not say "heart-sick" instead of "despairing"?
Why not say "despairing" instead of "depressed"?

Is there, perhaps, a quality in each person—hidden like a laugh inside a sob—that loves even more than it loves to live?
If there is, can it be expressed in the form of the lyric line?

Doestoevsky defended his later religious belief, saying of his work "Even in Europe there have never been atheistic expressions of such power. My hosannah has gone through a great furnace of doubt."

According to certain friends, Simone Weil would have given everything she wrote to be a poet. It was an ideal but she was wary of charm and the inauthentic. She saw herself as stuck in fact with a rational prose line for her surgery on modern thought. She might be the archetypal doubter but the language of the lyric was perhaps too uncertain.

As far as we know she wrote a play and some poems and one little prose poem called Prologue.
Yet Weil could be called a poet, if Wittgenstein could, despite her own estimation of her writing, because of the longing for a conversion that words might produce.
In Prologue the narrator is an uprooted seeker who still hopes that a transformation will come to her from the outside. The desired teacher arrives bearing the best of everything, including delicious wine and bread, affection, tolerance, solidarity

(people come and go) and authority. This is a man who even has faith and loves truth.

She is happy. Then suddenly, without any cause, he tells her it's over. She is out on the streets without direction, without memory. Indeed she is unable to remember even what he told her without his presence there to repeat it, this amnesia being the ultimate dereliction.

If memory fails, then the mind is air in a skull.

This loss of memory forces her to abandon hope for either rescue or certainty.

And now is the moment where doubt—as an active function—emerges and magnifies the world. It eliminates memory. And it turns eyesight so far outwards, the vision expands. A person feels as if she is the figure inside a mirror, looking outwards for her moves. She is a forgery.

When all the structures granted by common agreement fall away and that "reliable chain of cause and effect" that Hannah Arendt talks about—breaks—then a person's inner logic also collapses. She moves and sees at the same time, which is terrifying.

Yet strangely it is in this moment that doubt shows itself to be the physical double to belief; it is the quality that nourishes willpower, and the one that is the invisible engine behind every step taken.
Doubt is what allows a single gesture to have a heart.

In this prose poem Weil's narrator recovers her balance after a series of reactive revulsions to the surrounding culture by confessing to the most palpable human wish: that whoever he was, he loved her.

Hope seems to resist extermination as much as a roach does.

Hannah Arendt talks about the "abyss of nothingness that opens up before any deed that cannot be accounted for." Consciousness of this abyss is the source of belief for most converts. Weil's conviction that evil proves the existence of God is cut out of this consciousness.

Her Terrible Prayer—that she be reduced to a paralyzed nobody—desires an obedience to that moment where coming and going intersect before annihilation.
And her desire: "To be only an intermediary between the blank page and the poem" is a desire for a whole-heartedness that eliminates personality.
Virginia Woolf, a maestro of lyric resistance, was frightened by Freud's claustrophobic determinism since she had no ground of defense against it. The hideous vocabulary of mental science crushed her dazzling star-thoughts into powder and brought her latent despair into the open air.
Born into a family devoted to skepticism and experiment, she had made a superhuman effort at creating a prose-world where doubt was a mesmerizing and glorious force.

Anyone who tries, as she did, out of a systematic training in secularism, to forge a rhetoric of belief is fighting against the odds. Disappointments are everywhere waiting to catch you, and an ironic realism is always convincing.

Simone Weil's family was skeptical too, and secular and attentive to the development of the mind. Her older brother fed her early sense of inferiority with intellectual put-downs. Later, her notebooks chart a superhuman effort at conversion to a belief in affliction as a sign of God's presence.

Her prose itself is tense with effort. After all, to convert by choice (that is, without a blast of revelation or a personal disaster) requires that you shift the names for things, and force a new language out of your mind onto the page.

You have to *make* yourself believe. Is this possible? Can you turn "void" into "God" by switching the words over and over again?
Any act of self-salvation is a problem because of death which always has the last laugh, and if there has been a dramatic and continual despair hanging over childhood, then it may even be impossible.
After all, can you call "doubt" "bewilderment" and suddenly be relieved?

Not if your mind has been fatally poisoned. . . .
But even then, it seems, the dream of having no doubt continues, finding its way into love and work where choices matter exactly as much as they don't matter—at least when luck is working in your favor.

THE DESCENT

THE DESCENT

The descent has deepened
the interior lengthened

designated ending

Blind

pulled down inside and then
shot up again

to see east via the plateglass
a moon a monsoon an ashram

I used time almost wantonly
in that bald but sensual sky

to give me gusts
and more measurement

not to snap the stars shut
but Joseph said
you really ought

to tender how you sail by eye
your soul is just a length of baby

SOME DAY

Some day a sheep with green eyes will meet me
at a door

"Self, come in
and be as vigilant
as the alien you are."

I will enter with a book in my hand, I'm sure

. . . .

In secret space-time the heart is a conductor
who measures the length of a spirit's ride

"Heart, come along and be as heartless
as you know you are."

Red comrades inoperably close

I will follow with a book in my hand, I'm sure.

ANGRIA

When we were a baby
she fingered

my hood

like a fly
on the threads

of the dead

When she was a web
I fingered

her threads
like a spider

in love with a hand

A paper square
and noose-like letters

a floor that's a wall

so when I enter
I crawl

by my fingers and pen

O Angria so burn is the chill
to seek and hit

a place of guilt

where what is hot
is just the busy-work of thought

A grave-eaten parsonage
like its baby's lace cap

smells fertile. At first

the road away
across the heath turns like strings of DNA
But then there are no children

and no instruments
of mercy to help us carry on

Nothing happens that can

TARGETED

Three pointed arrows
and how they flew

front to back
breaking ice and glass

to burn and bite
and flutter here

where cuts bleed
until the feathers kill

THERE IS

There is a jail inside of me
it is a holy space
glove-filled for the individual baby

(a soul rewarded and destroyed)

Here like a frost of liquid nitrogen
the rain slides over the wires

in a thin water-cover

—one more fitting paler
for the real prisoners.

LET IT SNOW

Let it snow unless it is in heaven

Let it know
what it is itself that waterstuff

as it covers the silver
winter dinner bell

NO LIGHT

No light I can't
but let me write
of my dimensional other
mind ulterior

to the crux
of this huddle

while sheeted pilgrims
on autopsy tables
show a way

to when
under covers
of night-mist and apple

no holy talk confused them.

They just needed a place
to sleep with this

possible grain of light
buried deep
frozen to wet

(Or else was the thing
to "hang self in cell")

partially dying
like rain to mist

to graphic gray's

growth of myths

IS KNOWING

Is knowing the same as owning?
Do I already have it

(Poetic model)

a spiral thumb-print
taped responses
to each event

I thought I was
a five-part someone

who had to decipher the air
in things before navigating them

and each error was necessary

WINTER DISTANCES

Winter distances
form fir and snow

melting in points

Now a liquid yellow
is folding over

binding

—Krishna a leaf
when all these books are turf

THE CHILDREN TURNED

The children turned back to me
from eternity

uncertainly—notes a bird chipped off
natality repeating its stock

They were nearly human
And I was happy

to see a mouth in a face
not coldly attentive saying I think

but beings poured back
onto Baggage Street

each against the wall dreamily eating

AGAIN

When training to die
with your back to the train

you cry green green
to a blind Metropolitan

it means
you can't and you can

Then leap on the lap
of the tall blind man

who asks you to repeat

the word again

though now you're so beat you can't open your eyes to speak
or are you just unmanifest

NEVER

Never is going to be

soon enough for me

to say goodbye

so don't touch me
Who touched me

sorry but my head
would rather leave a thousand thoughts unsaid

than as air they would chill
in sunshine unpleasing

SOMEWHERE I HAVE NEVER

The hot costume
The hatchet surf

A lamb whose fleece was yellow
Gruff bald hills

And a bit of lightning
pinned on a pin

Will that light locate its sight
for my unborn being?

Save me from distressing?

Or lift from its dressing
my lastborn being?

UNDAY

From no nowhere not near the sea
on blue field flax
the cemetery's absolutely solitary
you and you and a third

of a pound of bread
for supper in the refectory
where I would die of hunger
if you—if soon—if on this unday—one

undoing would be undone

THE SOURCE

The source
I thought was Arctic

the good Platonic

Up the pole
was soaked film

an electric elevation
onto a fishy platform

and waves on two sides greenly welcoming

The sunwater poured on holy atheism

It was light that powered out

my ego or my heart
before ending with a letter

THE PASSION

I

Sun-blinded on a dark road
it must have been me that must have been he
if you stood there if you were where

I did as I guessed he would do

for me for never
without fear

would each approach the other so without eyes

Who of which one was the more winning
and who the colder and who the warmer

Who was my you or was it a you who was an ear
inclining to lips like the lips of someone else

pluraling as one into someone I missed

not you yes still you yes you: no you

I'd shed she'd shed she was shed
from the end of the land
eye looking one eye looking

hard of hearing hardly hearing
it was weard it was wierd it was weird
how he left no clues as to where

or whose you were anyway

it is both it was both
of us looking of her looking
of one looking at the other
the other's way

To see him from afar
no farther you farther you're farther no farther than when
you were not farther than this
from me than this here that there went on

At each turn we held on tight
as if in danger

—each error a correction

a hole in the air
so far
from the center

that a blooding together
of us feathers

world-heavy under the breast
and wheel

was necessary
for the homecoming

The grass that scents a man's skin
comes from the land where he was born and was one
    person
Ire as a beating wing, his dirty hands
But the bird and new-mown hay aren't with him now as
    linen, ash and I was.

Come back
to three lines of light on a little river—
one pink, one green and one aluminum—
come back to being

11

Where there was a current
but no currency

—wait, this didn't happen yet—

Where there was a current

on a sweet and salt lagoon
intersecting diameters

a painting of the place
hanging in my mind

gilding a frame for my rich
neurotic eros
there was someone like someone else

concocted extra-spatially
like a day's delivery of everything
past

and nothing to hope for
(but recollection)

the sky had the last word

It was imagination dying

Home is the water
I call home
blood thicker than brick
the river red with it

and walls supported
by spirits

When the marches and marriages
ended the days in jail

the way was work

In late night hours
work on the soul is the way

. . . but a third way
holds the second and the first
holds the third and all are called dark
when there is no work

Two children in winter
wheel and chill

in the silver carriage
in the stony town

"What would Father say
if he ever called?"

He'd be a quote from a book
with its solar jackets out of range

because that's where he stays

The dead do not converse
A snowlike still
A concrete sill
Squares squared everywhere

Blocked-in reflections
on windows gush
into suffering
figures in stainglass.

Those groans from the street
and the gruffness
of early Sunday's
pills and water

will get me to the railing

In the old way the old wood
gathered its shadows and twigs

but they wouldn't burn
They wouldn't burn

because of the ashes and ice
and the snapping

It was the month of red berries
and the brother and sister

held hands and ran
away laughing

III

Once on a summer night
in a humid tunnel

sex was scheduled

but no baby faces
looking up the time

pure lust
like a tulip

budding between our chests

—and it was fun!
—and I would do it again!

Blood when I dreamed of love

Love is the dream's blood

Blood on the way to the past

Red path red heart white dust

From the curling of a thumb
a plumb-line straight up

and out to its blue tip

with other woes we can't control or de-exist
pulled tight at the end of the stress

This is scattered I guess
to free the last

string of wishes
—given an easy term
and thankful too

for what I didn't get
in the same breath

as what manic I did

Was it luck or a plan
to call out alone

to spin a thread of spittle
as into a closed dark petal

The heart-mark (of love)
was a tulip
and the eyes of a pupil
a perfect cut
for someone
scarlet and doubtful

"What did you say to him?"
—Nothing. I loved him.

IV

A belly of snow
under a Moonday sun

a shiny cap a grimy cap

and the black
of a hedgerow of his and hers

sooty like fur

He was gray-complexioned
all the way down

the forest hall

Suits and coats
made out of smoke

formed holes for his arms to pass through

He managed his agony
but lost his looks and all his currency

For him time was a vacuum
filled with his visions

They held him above history
like valium

or something flat in heaven

He was always gone or leaving

claw-lines—white across a brick building—

A political laugh
flattened like linen

rolled apart
but still a haunt

Now strips of dust filter
over the prison
a man is leaving

Broken locks, and wood
that reeks of halfway cut
rotten books

Half a sun and half again
of it burning white

    "unhomelike"

I don't want his things to see me

Leave him hanging
Never call

His coat is open
His belt will fall

These are the actions
in hospital, woman or jail

When the camel's knees fold
it's the end of poetry

Hope-wired
to the purple
tulip in my heart

I should meet and not

hate this heavier knowledge
of terminal dates

let out my mind like mist
over the tree-tops

poetic stitch with
little dots to punch

on either side
of space and twigs

summer bunting
made out of nothing

but relationships

V

The shadow is an angel of a maybe

It travels like river water
on streets in the city—as much as
wherever things are pretty

I wish I could get it off of me or out
It's unbelievable
the way it doesn't see but feels me

Maybe this is addiction
Maybe a salvaging
Maybe I am shedding my skin or yours

(cold-covered skin trying to warm)

Maybe the angel is almost airborne
A woman who survived starvation
because her blood was so thin

I don't mean to be depressing
but I wanted to haul and wrap you
like a nibbled shark-white kin of mine

You flailed your way back into the engine

Don't you know what you've done
That was a soul you injured

It is now beyond weakness
It is adaptable

Heart pressed
in a book

—ink its hard
horrid

wordstain

engraved as a tulip
this heart cultivates

resistance

a culture
of powerful worms

At the transverberation
your heart is pierced

with such a piercing
you leave the sphere of doubt

Take heart
Lose heart!

Your heart is your tongue and the sweet jam that loves it
Your heart is your shoe, your place on the sod
Your heart is your baby cribbed in your ribs
Your heart is a tulip with a tulip-sign on it
Your heart is your brain
Your heart is a troubadour singing to wood
Your heart is a camel plodding along
Your heart is your ring that was reddish brown
Your heart is your sex and your mouth next to mine
Your heart is my heart that trails you in death
and guides me to the bird (a heart)
named Only-One-Song.

She put her hand
inside of his

and they held on
two wings on a bird

Then he let go
willing the sacrifice

to a little nest
at a higher position

"Give me a bucketful of colors
and not this melancholy gray memory"

If a goldfinch can pick up
a bucketful of water

with a tiny string, her mind
can lift her hope again

Shiny light that lives inside the skin

shining always shining
and the rain

An umbrella in the hall corner
signifies her brother's dream

He sleeps on the floor
under his raincoat

while the dog's tail thumps

Her ghost batted at the glass

She didn't understand
it wasn't her corporeal self
but her numinous inner body
that he had pinned to his chest
and the wires pulled on his skin
whenever he turned in bed

—the stains on the palms of his hands, red

The knees trembled but she touched the veins
and pulled the skin on that heart-extension

His little wounds, his dirty fingernails,
the beard he wouldn't clean and frayed hems,
the sunset cheeks and sweet skin,
smoke in his hair, himself
naked as a movie screen

Get out of this morass, poverty of spirit

She can't

Who names you but your teacher

The famine ended in a convulsion
of over-eating, then began the new fasting
Love everlasting as a vow of sex
Home abandoned for revenge

The children orphaned
until each dirty boy with rough nails
and wrists as soft as a girl's
became a man both rude and prudish

The sisters wrote about this
but only one of them never put quote-marks around the
    word love

He went astray
his pen tossed down
into a well
with a little stone splash

A bottle of bitters
became his system
Killing others
who died unwillingly

while he was killing
himself for fun

Every day was unday
for this one

There were no words
but winter nothingness
between piles of loving embraces
his legs curled in fear

VII

The wind drops
when the sun sets
A yellow cottage
A ceiling like curd

The west steps
into starriness

No comforter
No hand
to draw her on—

She hesitates—
stiff at the lintel—

"Gone again!"

Left bereft
by her/himself

but not died out to anyone yet

The winter skies are rough on wires
scratching on this twelfth night

Somewhere he's not calling

Near or far, before or behind
the erected cities

await the turning

since the dead precede the living
and also the becoming

Snow-moss silvers the trees

Its tint is cold
the way it sinks into a milk
and then joins a pallid scrim
over the skyline

Why does a heart wear its eyes
into hell
like slivers of false sunshine

The rented wall, the human back
heaving at the edge of the bed—

The spirit cried Here I am!
standing
with her hands held up
to greet him

Don't you see me?

Her brother
turned his back
and put her in the past

(blank-world
of the unable-to-have)

but her little fists pounded
out the ice cold tally

All will be well if only

One angel's efforts to cross the pond
Were long-limbed, winged in foam

Loved before, guided and ruined many
With a salt-slinging bow to history
Which stings, martyrs and burns

He didn't feel me

I hate therefore
The word "prayer"
Since every word is one

The angels must be laughing at paper
Crouched to examine the pink flower
Petals bending over a thorn and pen

VIII

In this grove there is only one patient. His heart like a berry
bleeds an aura onto ice-white sheets, his eyes glassy, his chest
cold. Even his tongue is cold.

He has eaten so much meat the beasts feel an affinity
and lick him where his heart is spilling. His eyes are lifted.

Nobody knows she is following him but he has left the light
on for her. She follows the imprint of his womanly feet.

Homeless he depends on his own arm to cover him
with his coat by closing it. Outside the wind chill
has brought the temperature down below zero.

His sisters wait at the night gate. One has eaten raspberries
from the patient's mouth.
The other is drinking the milky air.
"I was looking for you in some arcades."

The sky is merciful—a Virgin Universe. He has a thorn
on his brow as if he's a unicorn or Cain the woundable one.

Handbells ring: "Whose voice is this who laid to rest the fear
of being abandoned." He opens his johnny to show her the
evidence.

How does she know it is him when his throat and lips exist
somewhere else.
He might as well be a sleeping drunk in a war lobby or bar.

Up above, all is calm, all is clear.
"It came upon a midnight clear." The sound of one voice
speaking into some holes and coated wire.

"Oh shouts of stony light across the desert!"
A donkey's nostrils blow white air.

One hand freezing, one hand open, all her senses coiled
around the telephone. "I want to call someone please."
She is informed the line is free.

Now she can hear his laughter echo
through the plastic handset or is it a hand
banging a stone against a tongueless Celtic bell?

IX

I watched him disappear. This was the first station the one
where you can't believe what is happening
At first the sun shone like a dime and cinders
wouldn't stop falling until the last one flew up

Eyes cleared the light through the thin branches brittle
and un-birded. Red spots on ice. Dirt spots. Ashes
like feathers from seed-eating birds
who fly close to the ground

Across the harrowing span a pond would be ice and rough
like to die might be nice enough

His wings were a whole-cloth first
folded around his chest

so it hurt to rip apart
this revolutionary redbreast

and make him spread and fly

All his singing actually
was a cry of protest

Have lived!
Not this!
Have died!

The stations of my humiliation traveled
from telephone to telephone machine

Then I hit a knob and lost every message
to an illuminated blackness
A prayer reminds me of a telephone call

It represents the way the end of things
is on the ground

The ring comes whenever it will
because it's dark
where the mountains mother

and being stuck in one spot
is something to ring bells about

while the white goose travels
thousands of nautical miles

with one map and partner

I am giving you the most wonderful present
one memory can give another

a bridge of illusions

or snow as hard as the hood
of a car

Some people are radiators
even when their skin is thin and cold

Often they are drunk on memories

He for one carried a red bag by a string
to remember socialism
when he had no person to care for him

On his beat he went from ice to heated place

warming up the short space between lip and cup

To die for love
to die of love
to die in love
to die with love
to die over love
to die without love
to die to love
to die in the mine
and be a "mine"
in the arms of someone's
chest wound, "Here I will die of the above."

.

X

Some call it a desert though it's wet on the palate
Spiritual dryness makes reptile-faces

The scourge of vinegar bad wine bad guts
Who was laughed at and cut
and packed into a paddy wagon driven along the riverbank

and Officer Judas shouting, Lock him up!

This was after he'd exited the Mystic River bridge and before
either of us was d _ _ d

He said: *Put on your silks and follow me*

Blood rust on the cement
Cold dimpled cement. Rend your heart like your coat,
pull the lapels apart and show us the gash

Light-flattening, I forget

The belly's web and legs of a spirit-infested thing

I wear a single cross-beam I keep
forgetting like my own exhaustion

She's been hardened by a hard life
in public housing
where the rich keep the poor then rob them

Unfortunate girl always laughing

His legs were long and thin, his knees bent and feet crossed

I remember him stroking each one automatically

Soon he would be nailed
Agony, he begged

The temptation to suffer is a big quiet one
the kind that is generated by repetition

He got good at sleeping outside the same doors
and staring into the eyes of drivers-by

His empty pockets were stuffed with their glances

Rain and wind from the East River
to the blood red facade of Saint Veronica's

Two hands clasped in a car
Not an inauspicious start

The windowpane's a metaphor, not a force
but it won't let me have anything I want

So what is the relationship
between time and the soul?

Time has no temperature either

He slept on a plank, his blanket was air
He said he had never slept better

"We must die together."

Then I'll bear the torch and the needle
I'll carry and marry the ashes

They will be mine

I'll be the main mourner though no one will see me

I'll know why he died and what was the reason

Flowers attract scissors

XI

A decent soul comes in rum-red colors
It is a floating shadow
Not water or air but something nearly solid

A hint of cinnamon and bark

And some people know how to circle their lips
around a mouth and suck the soul away
just by leaning close taking hold
and tossing their legs around the person

You have to care for your soul
because time is transparent
and slides between you and your soul
when someone else has it

He is sipping my own
A binge of memories the color of raw sugar

It tastes delicious with the past

I left him I lost him
gone! The named
person the tall brother
untamed and shaking

We forgot to make plans
for this eventuality

No numbers or papers
I forgot to take
the vital information
from his raincoat pocket

since there was none
—only stray ends

The chest of a robin
reddened inedible

like the thorn-blood of Jesus
on the mouth where Judas kissed it
and made him into merchandise

The fallen angels folded their dirty wings
across their chests
and lowered their heads
to peck for oil as if they didn't notice

To the western wing of the Mayo clinic
she traveled to keep his back warm

Automatically
he raised the blanket

Useless jealousy

Either you're loved or you aren't

Skin icy, nipples bit, the little scrabbles and scores
His gums are sour grapes and those
whom he speaks to, clench their teeth

The plank in his eye is now on his back
It's awful the way he knows his mother waits
and weeps and it doesn't turn him

Pain-waves over the second station.
Women walk on the third through the tenth stations
Ground into light under the steam and steel.
Their keening like inexact wheels

Pain is the body's grinding
Pain sticks to the human brain
the way pollen sticks to a stamen

If you watch the man disappearing carrying his plank
you see dry splinters in the beginning
then just a cruciform as insignificant as a
broken-winged bird walking through a pit

XII

He swallowed my soul
so now I know
soul is physical
This was a test

Soul can be stolen
by a human kiss
A portion of soul
(I feel it missing)

Can it grow back
Can it fill in
the depression
dark and thin

an oil proportioned
to all skins, soul
now boldly bathing
in another's pool

Open him up and cut him apart
Hang him up, bind him with string
and you won't see him struggling
All heart he's lost his will, poor thing

Open him up and close him down
Let him live, he won't protest
Winter coats and wet hats
will never hang on him again

Open the door and let him out
into the sail-white winter night
Unhinged, unwinged, his coat
unbuttoned as he wants, poor thing

He was faithless but when it snowed
and she had the weather channel showing
blizzards where he lived
dread of his habitat seized her and held her
at needlepoint

His coat was ripped and who would sew it
Where would he find rest
when there was no name
for him at the cage and clinic, only
a convulsive overhang

of wind and snow splashing across the tarmac
and de-icing devices lifted to his wings, unbuttoned

Stations on the wall

fly past with vodka and milk
and a watchtower

Me and the self-loathing huddle together
averting our faces from each other

Time is breathing with us
when time is air

They could never have lived their lives together
But they did. Decades separated

By yards in the same time and town
Lost in probability.
Never meeting. Their souls were at source
one but addressed to some, intended for any, that lonely

In old age and young each liked to sleep
against something
The outer wall of a cathedral
The bend of a back
as if whispering:
"Six pennies and infirmity, never mention these."

XIII

I went by film to dreary high-rise apartment blocks.
Christmas lights and small cars. Wires still shimmered

in the air, windows like empty refrigerators

The man drove a cab as if he were dragging it

If you nail some white on a wall it turns yellow in time

Polar lilies and the gold spray of pollen
We invented film to see what we were doing

100% here, 100% there and 100% space between
In this triad is the whole stable machine

This angel clung to boats
and pecked at workers on their tits

It pissed and shat on their hair
as well as garden tents

Its song was repetitive

If the air around it wasn't soft
its feathers were

It preferred sugar-liquor to bread
and was Divine Mother's favorite

The mystery of preference
is never solved by acts

Sisters locked into the clasp of his bare legs without fear

He lay like John Lennon all over each one of them

In those days they didn't operate on babies
or have too many theories

Narcissism wasn't on the tongue though
other names for not knowing yourself by your own body
must have been

His father was an angel
Her mother man

The end of his line
Began with an organ

She carried her lyrics around in a bag
Along with some shoes and wings

Left one pair to pretend she was returning
But how could she?

Love is the movement towards perfection

I was hungry for love

It was pathetic the stones
I threw or smashed my mouth on
in my pathology of starvation

This hunger drove me
into the vineyards
with their drooping pebble-gray fruits

One mouth opened and sucked
out some of my love
Fermented mouth and tongue

I hung in the tree
of that one's torso and bones
It was the fruit I had been hunting

Not the cat or the worm

Not the feather-duster

Not the slime

Not the fowl or the fish

Not the birds of the air

None of them has a name

But amen

Amen in the dark

XIV

On the day I prayed
no one answered me
On the day I called
you didn't answer me

All the days I prayed
but there was a dial tone only
On the day you called
I was away

No self-pity
A week was made of six whole days
Seven was outside of them
A name a number an actual mean

Our souls need freedom
Otherwise price and kill
Or kiss and sell
Depend on it

The last image was a misprision.
Black-row of bristles and bird-broken snow
The old way, one pocket for two hands

A gash on his waterproof skin
The sole of a shoe open to the snow. Loss and dishonor

All this was really
a cement apartment block closed in for the people's dinner

He can't get back in
Terror is what

won't let him in
—terror squared

terror circled

He can't get back in

Please, Time
make a way!

Only the d _ _d
sleep outside

the arc of your caravan

Stick, sex, amoeba, outline, back

Stick, tucked
under the other's heart

and soil

Tender and unstuck

Wander, wander alone

The margin of error
now an aura—silver and slick
as a mirror

He didn't answer
The market crashed, rebounded
and the mourning doves cooed

He couldn't answer

Between my brain and this silence
time lifted and measured

There was no more reason to die

SHADOWS

1

It was still daylight
Seeing as the rim
Of the earth tended towards night
When she said the Messiah is turning
Let loose the demons from his cloth
And redden the ashes

(her psyche was shed)

The wind there was no wind
Unseparated from the one before

But when?
Not beatific not damned—

A float-heavy helium
That stirred the world
And its own intentions

Time began our limbo tree it grew
In brooding showers light and snow
Spirit in a watering can
Moisture of soul and verbiage
Now soil and verdure
Plant against chance

(The evanescent limb)

Get down on your knees God
And pray all cruelty
Ceasing—will—before
Your heart is for rent or sold
I know it's your heart
By knowing how it feels

(inside another)

2

The meat of an angel
Was chewed over supper
Demonic elements hovered
At table—center—cluster
Of probable beings
Unbottled

(Unacknowledged)

Rust-interrupted discharge
A loaf of flesh—as good as gone
Is all real stuff inching
Through Limbo's unfamiliar weather

(and language)

Two wings, now one
Space for cloth

3

He is felt as a feeling she feels him
She doesn't know why he to him being
Battle-catching mother
Whom she caught at the circulation
Still remembers
In her rose-lipped perceptor

(Love-thorn or birthing)

There is something between them

It climbs colorlike
The shades of pain
Describing their skins
Like a map's edge of ocean
It laps from her to him

They do feel that third person!

DESIGNER Nola Burger
TEXT 10/14.5 Scala
DISPLAY Joanna; Akzidenz Grotesk
COMPOSITOR BookMatters
PRINTER AND BINDER Friesens Corporation